National Zoological Park   Smithsonian Institution

National Zoological Park
Smithsonian Institution
Photographs by Jan E. Skrentny

Smithsonian Institution Press
Washington, D.C. 1976

CONTENTS

FOREWORD

This book attempts to tell our National Zoological Park story in pictures. The photos are as breathtaking as befits their wondrous subjects, our friends the wild species created to share this unique planet with us.

Many people now question whether zoos are needed any more. I think so, most vehemently. Zoos and their breeding-park adjuncts are the last chance that we will have of seeing a number of wild animals in the future.

The various wildlife trusts abroad have shown how threatened species can be preserved. Woburn Abbey saved Père David's deer as a munificent gesture. Peter Scott's Wildlife Trust helped to save the Hawaiian goose as an act of conservation philanthropy. The Jersey Wildlife Preservation Trust attempts to save a plethora of animal species.

Some management of breeding animal stocks may be the only way of saving various endangered species. In another fifty years most of the large terrestrial wild species will be gone, except for a few preserved by rational captive management. So captive breeding becomes an imperative.

The educational, scientific, and genetic potential of those animals that will survive is wholly in our own hands. It is a responsibility that far transcends public emotion or government regulation.

The Smithsonian's own National Zoological Park started out, as did most of the nineteenth-century zoos, as an instructive tool for the people, combining recreation and pleasure with a sense of wonder and awe at the lavish diversity of animal life around the globe.

Since World War II, zoo administration has come of age. Enthusiastic public interest in animals, fostered by the new worldwide perspective, has produced a generation of active zoo professionals who are eager to experiment away from the constraints of prisonlike concrete and steel cages and are concerned with captive rearing programs. This healthy new look has coincided with a tremendous surge of medical interest in animal pathology and animal behavior.

Now with our breeding-farm area of some 3,000 acres in nearby Front Royal, Virginia, more rare species can be bred in captivity and later exchanged with collaborating institutions. If these arrangements and others like them succeed, then zoological gardens will continue to delight and instruct the young and their parents with the fascination of a Noah's Ark.

With the new emphasis on reconstruction of the enclosures in Rock Creek Park, our Zoo bids fair to live up to its original hopes for instruction in the place and setting of animals and ourselves in our world, and we hope for the time in the near future when mankind will respect as never before his common inheritance in the beauty and diversity of nature, given to our charge in these closing days of the century.

S. Dillon Ripley
Secretary, Smithsonian
Institution

THE ROLE OF THE ZOO TODAY

In the end, we will conserve only what we love.
We will love only what we understand.
We will understand only what we are taught.
                    Baba Dioum, Senegal

The Zoo's mission is to present the beauty and
character of fellow beings in the animal kingdom so that
our and future generations of people, enriched by
personal discovery, will join in a commitment to cherish
and preserve life.
                    Edward Kohn
                    National Zoological Park

Smokey Bear, American black bear.

Hsing-Hsing, giant panda.

A HISTORY OF THE NATIONAL ZOO

Even before the Civil War, the Smithsonian Institution received gifts of live animals. But since there were little means with which to care for them, the animals were usually shipped to other zoos; a few were left to graze on the Mall in Washington. Gradually the collection grew.

Finally, in 1889 an act of Congress created the National Zoological Park. A headkeeper was hired and on June 15, 1890, the animals — consisting of 94 mammals, 61 birds, 5 snakes, 3 Galápagos tortoises, 17 alligators, 1 bullfrog, and an undisclosed number of water turtles — were moved from the Mall to the new Zoo in a borrowed wagon.

The early history of the Zoo was filled with problems and excitement. Just as it started, operating funds were cut in half, and to make things worse, the Zoo was expressly forbidden by Congress to spend any money buying animals. As a result, local donations became the major source of animals.

Circuses also provided animals. They also made special arrangements to winter their animals at the Zoo. In exchange for feed, the Zoo was allowed to exhibit the animal boarders, and also became the owner of any young born during that time.

The early Zoo was chronically shorthanded. Considerable difficulty was encountered in finding suitable men for positions as keepers. The starting salary was sixty dollars a month. Keepers came from farms, carnivals, and circuses. Most of them had a limited amount of schooling. Keepers were expected to feed the animals and clean their quarters, as well as mend fences, repair cages, and prepare food. Since there was no such thing as prepackaged foods, animal diets were mixed, ground, chopped, sliced, or baked — all by hand.

The first permanent Zoo structure was completed in 1891. It sheltered animals which needed heat during the winter and was named the "large animal house." Other construction was temporary — these paddocks, barns, and thatched-roof shelters remained for many years. The next permanent building was finished in 1907. It was planned as a small mammal house, but is now the Monkey House.

Then came the Depression, and the Zoo benefited from the federal recovery programs. Funds from the Public Works Administration were used to build the Reptile House, the Elephant House, the Small Mammal House, the restaurant, and shop areas.

The federal art programs of the thirties produced an array of new animals in stone and metal. Reliefs of prehistoric mammals grace the Elephant House; a bronze giant anteater stands in front of the Small Mammal House; and an assortment of stone beasts frame the Reptile House doorway.

The staff coped with the special problems of World War II, only to see the Zoo begin to lose ground afterward. Not until the 1960s was a plan designed and funded for the modernization of the Zoo.

In the spirit of the original Zoo plan, today's design emphasizes the beauty of the natural setting, but a century later it also means new ideas of increased space for animals and unobstructed views for visitors. Thus, the National Zoological Park has grown from its country beginnings to the present collection of animals and structures, changing always as new technology and information become available.

1912. Easter Monday: still one of the most popular days for visiting the Zoo.

7

Early construction at the Zoo.

9

In the early 1900s, scores of visitors to the Zoo strolled past rows of small cages whose occupants were tended by a small staff under the direction of the first headkeeper, William Blackburne.

ANIMALS ARRIVE AT THE ZOO

How do birds, mammals, reptiles, and amphibians from all over the world get to the National Zoo in Washington, D.C.? Many animals are born at the Zoo; others are donated, traded, or bought from other zoos or acquired from dealers. They come to the Zoo by airplane, truck, and car; but a traveling animal is rather an unusual passenger and cannot obtain protection, food, or water by itself—so these items must be amply provided.

Shipping animals is a delicate operation; there are almost as many kinds of crates, boxes, bags, and tanks as there are species. Large animals such as lions, tigers, and bears travel in crates with bars. Small rodents and birds make the trip in boxes with strong mesh screens. A venomous snake might arrive in a box labeled "DO NOT HANDLE"; within the box is loose packing material, and inside that is a cloth bag containing the snake. Crocodiles journey in long plywood boxes, elephants and rhinos in huge reinforced wooden crates, giant sea tortoises in water-filled tanks. A giraffe's trip to the Zoo in a wooden crate must be specially routed so that the towering head will clear all overpasses.

From time to time, the Zoo receives surprise gifts such as Smokey Bear, the giant pandas, and Mohini, the Zoo's first white tiger. In these special instances, the animals are personally accompanied. The pandas were escorted from China by two Peking Zoo keepers; Dr. Theodore H. Reed, Zoo director, went to India to accompany the white tiger to Washington.

Once an animal arrives at the Zoo, it is welcomed with respect and given the best treatment that scientific expertise and human caring can offer.

National Geographic Society

Dr. Reed, director of the National Zoo, journeyed to the palace of the Maharajah of Rewa in India, to select the Zoo's first white tiger. The tiger he chose was a female named Mohini, which means "enchantress."

A simple method was used to move Mohini into her shipping crate. The cage with food inside was placed in her enclosure. At first she was wary, but later entered and the door was tripped shut behind her.

Porters carried Mohini from the palace to a truck which made the long, dusty journey to the airport.

Mohini was watched over carefully throughout the long flight to the United States.

Dr. Reed describes his experience choosing the white tiger: "To me, the big thrill was opening the barred doorway to the harem courtyard at the palace, and there was Mohini with the other white tigers. Her coat was a beautiful white, with no hint of yellow. She was curious, sniffing at us. She actually selected *us*: she was the most heads-up-alert, interesting animal."

THE PANDA STORY

Hsing-Hsing and Ling-Ling, the Zoo's male and female giant pandas, came to the United States in 1972 as a gift from the people of The People's Republic of China. Twenty years had elapsed since these black-and-white favorites had been seen in the Western Hemisphere, although their closest relatives, the lesser pandas, had already been known to Zoo visitors for years.

Ling-Ling was 18 months old and Hsing-Hsing was 12 months old when they made their 11,800-mile journey to Washington aboard an Air Force cargo plane. Their arrival on a drizzly April dawn was an exciting international milestone which sparked the curiosity of millions of people. Weeks before, the Zoo's curators, keepers, researchers, and veterinarians were planning a comfortable, permanent home for these rare and special animals.

The house that awaited them was carefully redesigned, using knowledge of the pandas' needs both in the wild and in captivity. The inside enclosure is kept at a constant 60 degrees, much cooler than the public viewing area, because the natural setting to which the pandas are accustomed is the rhododendron-and-bamboo forests of the Chinese Himalayan Mountains. Sleeping dens built between the enclosures provide the pandas complete privacy during resting times.

The yards are a playground for the pandas year-round. As long as the temperature stays below 70 degrees, the pandas seem comfortable outside; but once it becomes warmer, they are let back indoors. In summer, their outdoor activity occurs usually between 8 A.M. and 9 A.M.

Giant panda.

The giant pandas eat a special diet, developed by the Zoo staff. Twice daily, keepers feed them bamboo, whole raw apples and carrots, cooked sweet potatoes, rice gruel with honey, and dog biscuits, as well as vitamins. Sometimes they treat them with a bread-and-honey sandwich. Keepers watch the pandas' eating and report any changes in habits to the curator. In addition, Hsing-Hsing and Ling-Ling are weighed each month.

Bamboo is a fast-flowing commodity at the Zoo: the pandas eat a total of 40 to 50 pounds of it every day! This poses a major problem. How can the Zoo come up with 350 pounds of bamboo a week? Some of the supply is cultivated at the Zoo, but it is not enough. Fortunately, ornamental bamboo is grown in many backyards in Washington, D.C., and the Zoo gets hundreds of calls a year from people willing to donate some for the pandas.

Panda care involves other health aspects: worming them (worms such as tapeworms and roundworms are common parasites); immunizing them against such diseases as distemper and hepatitis; and cleaning their enclosures daily — all of which keep disease-producing organisms at a minimum.

Many visitors wonder why the giant pandas are separated from one another. This practice is based primarily on knowledge of panda behavior in the wild, where they are solitary and come together only to mate. When Ling-Ling is in heat, she and Hsing-Hsing are allowed to share an enclosure, play with each other, and possibly breed.

The giant panda is not a   17
bear. After a thorough
investigation, scientists
both in China and at the
Smithsonian Institution are
convinced that it belongs
in a family of its own along
with the lesser panda.

Since the presence of these animals in captivity is extremely rare, and none have been born in the Western Hemisphere, breeding the giant pandas is one of the Zoo's important concerns. Giant pandas have one and occasionally two breeding seasons a year; the female comes into heat in the spring and sometimes in the fall. Curators know at about what time the breeding season occurs and a "heat watch" is begun. When Zoo staff confirm that the female is actually in heat, the pandas are put together.

The pandas' breeding season is a time brimming with Zoo activity. During the encounter, researchers, curators, and keepers document the pandas' breeding behavior. Some bring 35-millimeter and movie cameras or videotape equipment. Others come with pens and notebooks, and still others carry tape recorders. All of these methods produce a complete record of the encounter. Without a doubt, the arrival of a cub (or cubs!) belonging to Ling-Ling and Hsing-Hsing would certainly be an event celebrated throughout the world.

You might expect the lesser panda to look simply like a smaller version of its black-and-white cousin. But no — it is reddish-brown and creamy white, with a tear-stripe on its cheek and a long, ringed tail. The breeding of lesser pandas at the Zoo has been quite successful:

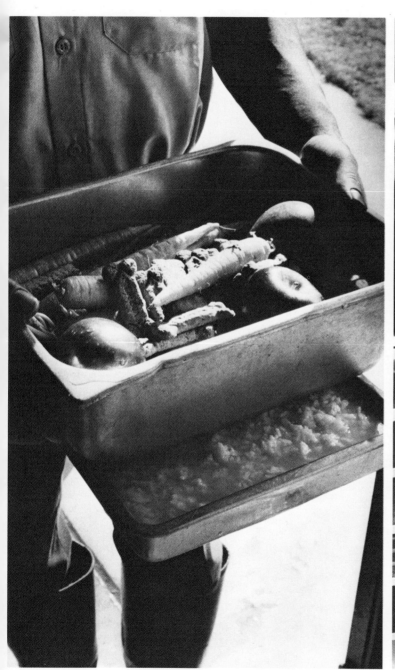

Keepers search throughout the Washington area for isolated patches of bamboo, preferring plants which are tender and uncontaminated by pollution. Each week they harvest hundreds of pounds for the pandas to eat.

Gathering up food for all the Zoo's animals is a full-time job for the Zoo's commissary staff. Some foods, like fresh fruit, vegetables, and horsemeat, are quite easy to obtain, while others, like crickets and mealworms, are more difficult to supply. Some, like tender young oat shoots, are grown at the Zoo by efficient hydroponic methods.

20

The giant panda's natural diet is simulated in the meals prepared at the Zoo. Included for each panda are up to 30 pounds of bamboo a day, as well as fruits and vegetables.

Sometimes blocks of ice, weighing up to 500 pounds, are given to the pandas during the hot summer months. The ice blocks provide great amusement for both pandas and visitors.

Every morning crews of maintenance workers wash down the walkways and clean up the Park long before the first visitor arrives.

Police, carpenters, and welders are a few of the many workers whose support keeps the Zoo running on a day-to-day basis.

Giant pandas are solitary
animals in the wild and
come together only to
mate. At the Zoo, the
pandas' enclosures are
separated; during mating
times the two animals are
put together.

Volunteer guides,
recruited by the Friends of
the National Zoo (FONZ),
are stationed in various
buildings to answer
questions and provide
interesting information
about the animals.

Hsing-Hsing and
Ling-Ling meet at the
moon gate separating
their enclosures.

many young have been born. Reproduction has been encouraged by the provision of several nesting boxes to which the mother can move and hide her cubs — allowing her to raise her young, just as she would in the wild; and also by the isolation from the public of the enclosure after the birth of cubs, in order to protect their privacy.

Visitors are well aware of the concern and responsibility the Zoo staff have for the pandas. But this is just a highlighted example of the good daily care, nutrition, and surroundings provided all of the animals at the Zoo.

New quarters for the lesser pandas' growing young require a move. The panda is caught in the keeper's net, transported in a box, and released in the newly planted enclosure. Everyone gets great pleasure watching the panda first explore, then settle down in its new home.

The lesser panda moves her cubs from one nest to another as she does in the wild. Often a keeper must search every nesting site in an enclosure to find the cubs so that they can be checked and weighed.

The tiny cubs of the lesser panda do not acquire their parents' reddish coloring until four months old, when they shed their baby fur.

A VARIETY OF ANIMALS

When the last individual of a race of living things breathes no more, another heaven and another earth must pass before such a one can be again.

William Beebe
First Curator of Birds
New York Zoological Park

Greater kudu with young.   29

Mandarin duck.

Dorcas gazelles with young.

Nile hippopotamus with young.

Old World pelicans preening.

Australian black swan.

South African shelduck.

Crowned crane.

African lion.

33

Indian elephants with trainer.

Sable antelope.

Red kangaroo.

Jaguar.

Geoffroy's cat.

Cuban crocodile.

Red uakari.

European brown bear
cubs.

Black rhinoceros.

Lowland gorilla.

Meerkat. 39

Prairie dog.

Indian peafowl.

Coscoroba swan.

Spectacled bear.

Water dragon.

Binturong.

Polar bear.

Wood duck.

Masai giraffes.

Burmese brow-antlered deer.

FROM EGG TO HATCHLING

In nature, birds and reptiles select where and how their eggs are incubated. Birds generally lay their eggs in a nest and keep them warm and protected. Those reptiles that lay eggs commonly deposit them in secluded places, buried in the soil or under mounds of leaves, where they are left to develop without parental attendance. The proper incubation conditions often determine whether eggs will hatch.

In captivity, an animal's choices are somewhat limited and eggs may often be neglected or destroyed by the parent. It is for this reason that the Zoo frequently takes over nature's role and incubates eggs artificially.

Hatching bird eggs in captivity is a refined and systematic science, whereas hatching reptiles is left more to experimentation and guesswork. Man's experience raising birds and cultivating their eggs spans many centuries, and birds' nesting habits are often easily observable in the wild. In contrast, raising reptiles has not been nearly so readily practiced, and reptile reproduction is much less understood because of their secretive habits. Also, in captivity, fewer reptile eggs are laid than bird eggs; thus, there is a more limited source of experience from which to learn.

At the Zoo, bird and reptile keepers make their rounds each morning and search the enclosures for eggs laid during the night. They usually remove the eggs and carry them to the incubator room. Here a careful routine

American bald eagles. 43

Giant day gecko.

The gecko lays two joined eggs which stick to vertical surfaces such as this bamboo stalk.

A keeper checks birds' eggs in the incubator. Numbers penciled on shells identify species and date incubation began.

is followed. In the Bird House, a technician disinfects and identifies the egg and pencils the species name, identification number, and date on the shell. Knowing what species the egg came from is important in determining such incubation conditions as length of time, temperature, and relative humidity. The egg identification information, including the date the egg was laid and the date it was placed in the incubator, is logged into a record book. These records, like ones kept in the Reptile House, aid in predicting when each egg is due to hatch. Careful documentation helps keep track of the thousands of eggs that birds and reptiles lay at the Zoo in a single year.

The incubators in the Bird House are large automatic machines which turn the eggs at least three times a day. Incubation is based on workable, proven formulas for each species of egg. In contrast, since knowledge of reptile egg-laying is sketchier, the Reptile House has a rather curious array of incubation equipment which reflects a varied and sometimes experimental approach. One kind of improvised incubator is a gallon jar filled with dampened sand and warmed by a light bulb suspended over the opening. There are many variations of this style, made from containers of assorted shapes and sizes, and filled with different kinds of bedding material such as peat moss or pea

The American bald eagle, 45
whose existence is
threatened in the wild, has
bred at the National Zoo.

To achieve successful
breeding, the eagles were
given a large flight cage
for their exclusive use,
since they would not mate
when other birds shared
the cage.

46

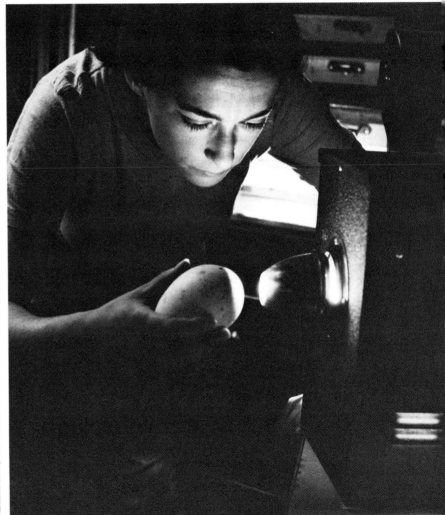

Baby Carolina wrens are hand-fed mealworms.

A hatchling has just emerged from its egg.

"Candling" an egg is an effective way to determine if it is fertile. Once hatched, the young bird is hand-reared.

The large aviary affords room for this adult bald eagle to fly.

gravel. Small automatic incubators, designed for bird eggs, have also been tried.

Once the bird or reptile egg is in the incubator, a keeper checks the incubation conditions periodically and "candles" the egg in order to monitor the embryo's development.

Hatching at the Bird House is a rather routine, predictable occurrence. With reptiles, however, it is more chancy. In spite of constant attention many reptile and some bird eggs do not hatch. To determine why nothing happened, the keeper checks to see if the egg was fertile; if so, how far the embryo had progressed; and what factors might have prevented its growth. From cases of unsuccessful incubation, the Zoo staff can learn ways to increase future hatching success. But to expect all eggs to hatch is an unrealistic goal, since even in the wild there will always be a percentage that do not develop.

Once able to live on their own, the healthy young birds and reptiles may be added to the Zoo's collection or may be sold, loaned, or traded to other zoos.

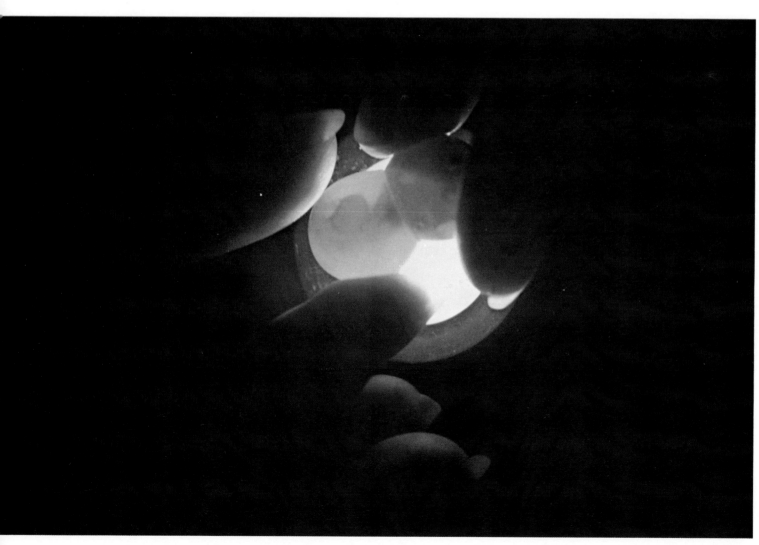

The eggs laid by the gecko will soon be removed from the animal's enclosure and transported to the incubator room.

A keeper records identifying data into the logbook.

A keeper "candles" a gecko egg and sees the outline of the developing embryo inside.

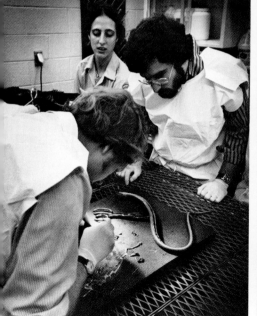

The newly hatched gecko is almost self-sufficient, as are most reptiles.

Corn snakes and eggs.

The death of an animal at the Zoo, in this case a glass lizard (a legless species), demands that an autopsy be performed. The autopsy reveals valuable information which can influence aspects of daily care and benefit future generations of reptiles. Keepers and students attend the autopsies to further their knowledge of the animal.

A keeper prepares food for the animals in the Reptile House.

"FOR THE ADVANCEMENT OF SCIENCE"

Research and continuing learning about animals occur
in nearly every phase of Zoo activity. A reptile keeper
watches and notes the behavior of newly arrived Cuban
crocodiles and perhaps applies these observations
toward a special project. The curator of mammals might
analyze the breeding behavior of cheetahs or lesser
pandas. Research zoologists, biotechnicians, and
veterinarians tackle long-range projects dealing with
topics from anesthesia to nutrition to social
development.

This research is not a new element of the Zoo's
function. In fact, research was directly stated in the
1889 Congressional mandate by which the Zoo was
established: ". . . for the advancement of science, and
the instruction and recreation of the people."

Tucked away on a wooded hillside in Rock Creek Park
is a Zoo building few visitors ever see. Like the public
exhibit area, this facility houses such diverse animals
as monkeys, rodents, and birds. This place has a very
special purpose. Here, research about animals
continues at nearly all hours of the day and night. The
resulting knowledge is a valuable key to understanding,
maintaining, and breeding exotic animals in captivity.

An off-exhibit facility is very important, because it
allows zoologists to work closely with animals.
Off-exhibit, more of one species can be kept for
breeding purposes, whereas on-exhibit at most one or
two pairs can be on view. Thus, a genetically viable
population can be maintained in the Zoo.

A revealing glimpse into what goes on here can be
seen in the case of the golden marmoset. This small,

Spider monkeys nestle together for warmth and protection.

Wooden beams, such as the one on which this howler monkey relaxes, are designed to be an abstract version of a treetop habitat. They provide an opportunity for natural movement.

A golden marmoset screeches a warning to would-be poachers of its food. Studies of marmoset vocalizations are part of research projects conducted by the Zoo.

striking primate is so highly endangered in the shrinking coastal jungles of Brazil that only 400 to 600 remain. At the Zoo, a series of research projects are providing more complete understanding of the golden marmoset's social and sexual behavior and development. These studies have yielded a very important finding: that marmoset parents "train" juveniles to care for infants and thus prepare them for parenthood. For example, juveniles help their fathers carry the infants and return them to the mothers for feeding. When the juveniles become parents, they are already accustomed to being around newborn infants and to carrying them, and thus are able to rear their own young. Researchers have learned that without this prior exposure to infants, for a minimum of three weeks, new parents will often reject their infants and even bite or kill them. This shows the importance of leaving marmoset family groups together. With conclusions drawn from the data in all of these studies, Zoo researchers hope to improve the breeding success and care of this rare animal.

Other primates are also subjects of research and curiosity. In one nine-year project, a Zoo scientist has studied auditory communication among spider monkeys. The researcher was particularly interested in how vocalizations develop in the young and reach adult expression; such insight might enhance understanding of the development of human communication. To test the role of learning in the use of adult vocal patterns, young spider monkeys were reared in isolation from their parents and their vocalizations analyzed. The scientist found that these sounds were like those of the parents; the vocalizations had developed entirely without imitative learning.

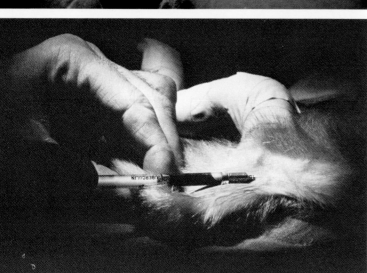

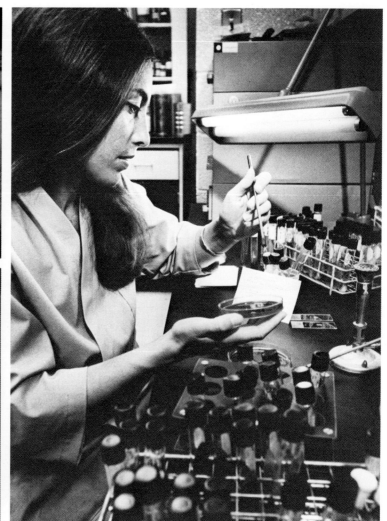

The Zoo's research projects on the endangered golden marmoset involve daily observations and recordings of its behavior. Such research leads to understanding of the golden marmoset's social and breeding patterns—and more golden marmosets.

After setting the fractured leg of a marmoset, the veterinarian takes a sample of blood from the anesthetized animal for laboratory analysis as part of a special study to determine effects of anesthesia. Studies like this will help veterinarians in zoos across the country to better administer safe doses of anesthesia to sick animals.

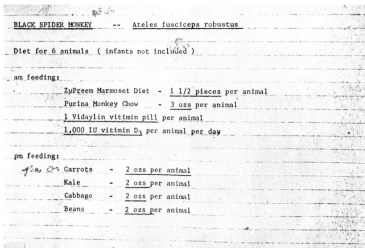

BLACK SPIDER MONKEY -- *Ateles fusciceps robustus*

Diet for 6 animals (infants not included)

am feeding:

ZuPreem Marmoset Diet - 1 1/2 pieces per animal
Purina Monkey Chow - 3 ozs per animal
1 Vidaylin vitimin pill per animal
1,000 IU vitimin D_3 per animal per day

pm feeding:

Carrots - 2 ozs per animal
Kale - 2 ozs per animal
Cabbage - 2 ozs per animal
Beans - 2 ozs per animal

A new animal enclosure is the result of months of collaboration among keepers, educators, zoologists, designers, and builders. Small-scale models of the projected design enable potential problems to be identified and remedied. The materials used in construction of the enclosure must be durable enough to withstand the monkeys' vivacious activities.

A keeper observes the spider monkeys in their new enclosure.

Preparing the monkeys' special diet and keeping the enclosures clean are part of a keeper's job.

Thousands of miles away from the Zoo's research center in Rock Creek Park, field scientists are involved in another Zoo project. In the dry tropical grasslands and humid jungles of Venezuela, these people are studying the red howler monkey, moustached wren, rice rat, cebus monkey, giant and lesser anteaters, and a species of pond turtle. Projects focus on the role of key vertebrate species in both habitats, as well as on such aspects as their abundance, feeding preferences, and population dynamics.

The findings from these field studies can be applied toward the housing, care, and breeding of certain animals which are difficult to maintain in captivity, such as anteaters and howler monkeys.

Research, both in the field and at the Zoo, is a very valuable resource for enhancing understanding and improving care of the Zoo's animals. To contribute to the health and perpetuation of a thriving animal community is one of the many gifts zoological research can make.

These baby monkeys—a spider monkey and a golden marmoset—are the result of the Zoo's conscientious research and breeding programs.

In the rain forests and tropical grasslands of Venezuela, zoologists conduct research. Part of the project includes population studies which require capturing, marking, and releasing of small mammals, such as the opossum.

A giant anteater, rescued from a ditch where it had fallen, is examined before its release by a Venezuelan conservationist and a research scientist from the National Zoo.

South American pond turtles caught in traps are marked and released, after which their wanderings can be monitored.

ANIMAL HEALTH

The health care of the animals in the Zoo is a complicated and full-time job. There are over 2,000 different inhabitants whose physical forms and modes of life may not be at all alike. These animals, unlike human beings, cannot describe their symptoms to a doctor. With many exotic species, there are no precedents for dealing with their medical problems. To further complicate matters, many animals are not tame and are very difficult to handle when sick.

Keeping the animals healthy involves the whole Zoo, but requires primarily the constant energies of a specialized animal health staff, including a veterinarian, interns, a pathologist, and laboratory technicians working within a modern animal hospital.

The main objectives of the animal care program are preventive medicine and early diagnosis. Keepers watch the animals and report any problems — even minor ones — to the curators, who alert the veterinarian. He decides what needs care immediately and what can be postponed until his regular rounds. Each day the veterinarian travels throughout the Zoo, treating the sick and discussing health care with curators and keepers. Daily duties are varied. He might give an injection to a monkey, trim the overgrown hoof of a zebra, treat a wound on a monitor lizard, or show a keeper how to administer medication to an animal. Animals in need of continuous, specialized care might be taken back to the hospital.

The veterinarian and his staff also set time aside to attend to projects, such as surgery. A hernia in a monkey requires repair or the frost-bitten tail on an

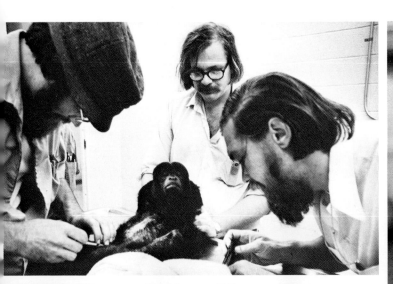

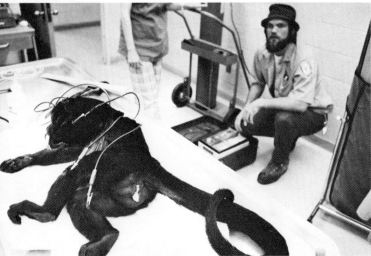

Dental checks provide clues to an animal's general physical condition.

The veterinarian and his staff practice preventive medical care. Whenever possible, animals are given regular physical examinations, which include tuberculin skin tests, blood studies, and X rays. Often keepers and research zoologists participate in these examinations.

Animals, just like human beings, are wired for electrocardiograms. The results give the veterinarian a printed pattern of the heartbeat.

The howler monkey returns to his enclosure.

anteater necessitates amputation. There are diagnostic exams to be given: a pregnancy test for an orangutan, X rays to determine if a broken limb has knit properly, or an electrocardiogram for a howler monkey. There are also regular tests to be made, like the primate TB screening program. Finally, there are research projects to pursue, to answer some puzzling questions, such as how much of a certain antibiotic can you administer to a snake?

Sudden emergencies are a fact of life for the health staff, and frequently disrupt the day's — and sometimes the night's — plans. An antelope, in an unexpected encounter with a cagemate, crashes into a fence and breaks a leg; a giraffe gives birth; or a monkey aborts an expected young. A call from the animal department rouses the veterinarian. He gathers up the equipment and people he will need to help, and rushes off to the scene of trouble. After treatment, the patient will be checked each morning when the veterinarian makes his rounds.

In all his work, the veterinarian collaborates closely with the pathologist and laboratory staff. Routinely, the pathologist performs autopsies on every animal that dies at the Zoo, in order to determine the cause of death and other health problems the animal might have had. He looks for obvious reasons for death, such as parasites, internal injuries, and diseased organs. Representative tissue samples from all organs and from the diseased areas are collected for laboratory analysis.

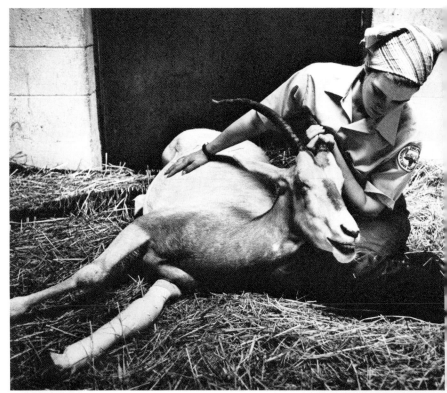

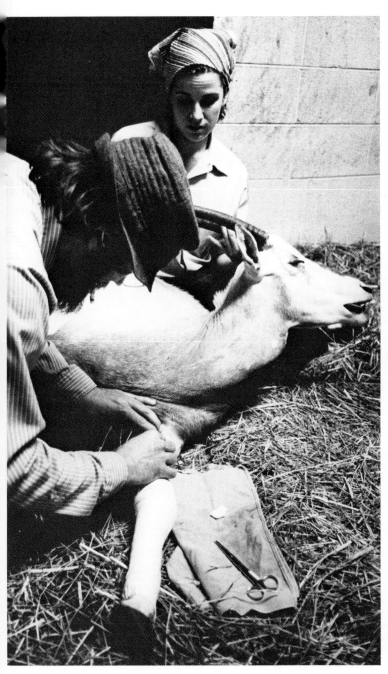

When a scimitar-horned oryx suffered a gash in its left foreleg, members of the health division hurried to administer first aid. A keeper held the sedated oryx while the veterinarian bandaged its leg and took a blood test.

After healing, the oryx was sedated, crated, and transferred to the Zoo's Conservation and Research Center near Front Royal, Virginia. It was left in its crate to awaken and join the herd of oryx already there.

Information gained from the autopsies is shared with the veterinarian and curators and applied to help insure the health of the living animals in the collection. For example, the autopsy of a gecko lizard with soft bones revealed a calcium deficiency. To prevent this occurrence in the remaining geckos, the staff decided to fortify the diets with a calcium supplement.

Another major task for the Zoo's laboratory staff is to analyze specimens, such as fecal and blood samples, collected from the living animals. Technicians look for signs of parasites or other sicknesses which help the pathologist determine what an animal's problem might be.

Just as with human health care, careful medical records and case histories are kept in the hospital for all the animals treated in the Zoo. These records, plus the accumulated experience of the Zoo staff, result in a growing fund of knowledge that produces increasingly better medical care for all the animals in the Zoo.

The Conservation and 67
Research Center provides
animals space to roam
freely with little human
intervention.

THE CONSERVATION AND RESEARCH CENTER

In the shadow of the Blue Ridge Mountains in Virginia, 75 miles from the National Zoo, tire skids on the roadside mark the startled reactions of motorists to zebras grazing in the fields nearby.

Zebras? In Virginia? Yes. For this is the Zoo's new Conservation and Research Center at Front Royal: 3,150 acres of rolling foothills, pastures, forests, and barns are home to herds of scimitar-horned oryx, Père David's deer, Burmese brow-antlered deer, zebras, onagers, Bactrian camels, rheas, cranes, maned wolves, and others.

Throughout the century, the property has housed several government-sponsored, animal-breeding programs. From 1909, the Army's Remount Depot raised horses and mules for the cavalry, until jeeps took over. The War Dog Reception and Training Center was added in 1942. Six years later, the Department of Agriculture acquired the land for a Beef Cattle Research Station. Transfer of the site in 1975 to the Smithsonian Institution achieved the Zoo's aim for a permanent site for long-range breeding programs.

The Zoo's Conservation Center was created to sustain gene pools of rare and endangered species of mammals and birds, using modern breeding practices based on research; and to share this knowledge with the rest of the world. The need has never been greater. For many species, urban zoos can rarely devote the space needed for effective breeding; importations of wild animals into the United States shrink, as do their numbers in the vanishing wilds.

Why is space essential? Because the long-term breeding success of many species requires that their natural social organization be allowed. Take the Père David's deer, for example. A city zoo, at best, can hope to house only a single male and a small group of females. At the Center, space is available as well for a much larger group of females, their young, and a bachelor group, all contributing to the success and vitality of the herd of Père David's deer.

Intensive study involves every program at the Center, from learning land use for exotic species, to determining the best ways to breed endangered animals. Every species has its own needs which must be understood if its occupancy on earth will be shared with man in decades to come. This is what the Center is all about — an effort joined by zoos around the world to secure precious life forms for future generations.

In the words of Dr. Theodore H. Reed, director of the National Zoo: "In the future, perhaps 50 years from now, the Center in Front Royal might be more important to the total life of zoos in the United States and to conservation and the study of animals, than this Zoo or any other. The Center gives us promise of being able to perform our welcomed responsibility to act as a proper host to fellow members of the animal kingdom. They are ambassadors to our cities. Our charge is to interpret their language and share their ages-old story with all who care to listen. But first we must preserve their lives, so that tomorrow we can hear their voices."

Acres of rolling countryside afford Père David's deer the liberty to wander and establish herds. Originally from China and now extinct in the wild, the Père David's deer are flourishing in the hills of Virginia.

Deep forests provide browsing grounds and a hiding place for the bongo. They also present a challenge to the animal staff, who must search the woods every day to locate members of the herd.

The bongos in their large enclosures do not feel threatened and will permit close approach by the keepers.

Even with the aid of four-wheel drive, vehicles can get bogged down in low, swampy places or stuck on unseen boulders, miles from help.

To protect the animals from predators, 8-foot-high chain link fences were erected. These barriers must be inspected daily for holes dug underneath and damage caused by fallen branches; repairs are made as soon as possible.

Rheas from South America and Bactrian camels from Asia now thrive near Front Royal, Virginia.

Using videotape cameras to record activity and computers to compile the information, researchers study the encounter behavior of South American maned wolves.

Grant's zebra graze on the hillside.

Two young Père David's deer watch the herd's activity from a distance. Someday these bucks will challenge the herd master, the strongest male deer, for supremacy over the females.

The Center furnishes a setting which encourages natural behavior. A male zebra issues a challenge to other males for dominance over the herd.

Oryx come from desert areas of the Middle East, but like other species at the Center, they have adapted to green Virginia pastures.

California sea lion.

Roloway guenon.

Cheetah.

Volunteer tour guide with a local school group at the cheetah exhibit.

White Bengal tiger.

Additional Photo Credits

Pages 7-9, National Zoological Park Archives; 10-13, Robert Abercrombie, National Geographic Society; 16, panda on bridge, Robert E. Mulcahy; 17, panda portrait in snow, Jordan D. Ross; 23, panda eating carrot, Max Hirshfeld; 28, kudu and young and 29, hippo and young, Pat Vosburgh; 39, water dragon, Max Hirshfeld; 44, eagle and young and 46, Carolina wrens, Pat Vosburgh; 60, Venezuela morning, Judith White; 60, opossum, Dale Marcellini; 60, red howler monkey, John Eisenberg; 61, giant anteater, Ken Green; and 61, turtles, researcher in water, Dale Marcellini.

Designed by Robert E. Mulcahy

Written by the Office of Education, National Zoological Park, with thanks to the rest of the staff.

80

First edition

Printed in the United States of America
by Stephenson Lithograph

Library of Congress Cataloging in Publication Data
    Washington, D.C. National Zoological Park.
    ZOOBOOK.
    1. Washington, D.C. National Zoological Park.
I. Skrentny, Jan E.   II. Title.
QL76.5U62W376 1976   596'.0074'0153   76-9653
ISBN 0-87474-846-1
ISBN 0-87474-845-3 pbk.

Cover: White Bengal tiger. Photograph by Max S. Hirshfeld